I give thanks to my many teachers and guides:
Hawayo Takata, Amorah Quan Yin, Eric Vormann, Judith
Lynne, Chogyam Trungpa, Patrick Zeigler, Janelle Kaye,
Genai Ellen Wachs, as well as to my beloved family.

—Margot

For Phil, Maggie, Hayden and Henry.

—Ari

Balboa Press books may be ordered through booksellers or by contacting:

Balboa Press
A Division of Hay House
1663 Liberty Drive
Bloomington, IN 47403
www.balboapress.com
1 (877) 407-4847

ISBN: 978-1-5043-6960-2 (sc)
ISBN: 978-1-5043-6961-9 (e)

Library of Congress Control Number: 2016918816

Print information available on the last page.

Balboa Press rev. date: 11/16/2016

BALBOA.
PRESS
A DIVISION OF HAY HOUSE

WHAT COLOR MAKES YOUR HEART SING?

Written by Margot Vance-Borland

Illustrated by Ari Vance-Borland

Some people come on the blue wave.
They love oceans and sky and blueberries
in the summer. They like to lie on their
backs and look up at the blue, blue sky.

Some people come on the green wave...
nourished and fed by the green hillsides
and trees. Standing in the forest with bright
green sprouts poking out of the ground.

Some people come on the pink ray...
they love roses and little pink flowers
that line the path where they dance.
When they see pink, they feel happy inside....

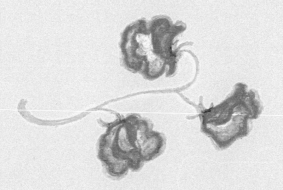

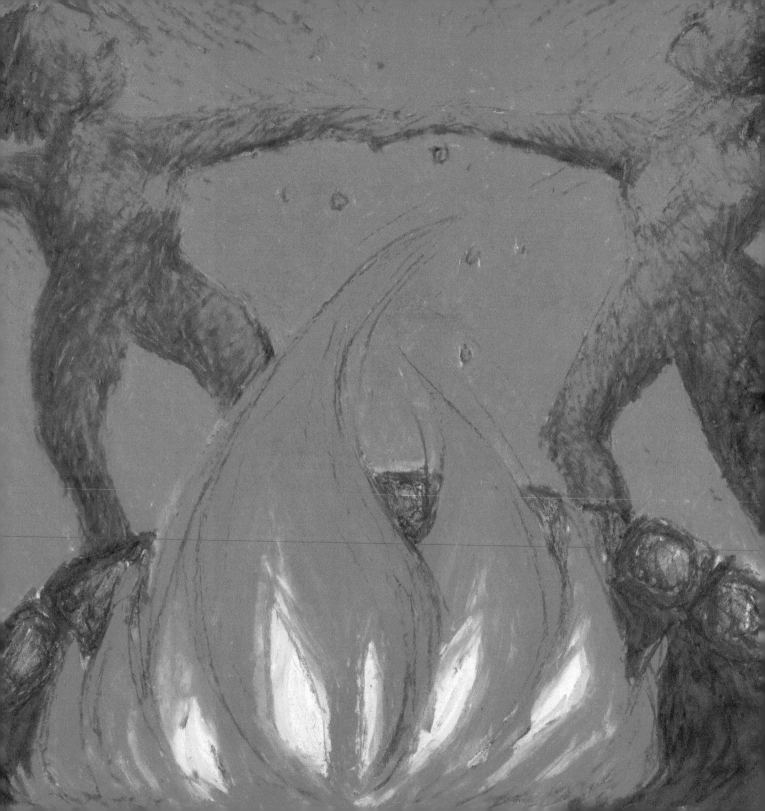

Some people like red...fiery and powerful
and bursting with energy.
Enough energy to fire the universe.

Some are children of the orange ray...
alive and vibrant like the sun at sunset,
and the brightly falling leaves of autumn.

Some people like yellow...
warm and glowing and filled with light.
They have smiles on their faces
and a golden glow that fills up their hearts
with warmth and laughter.

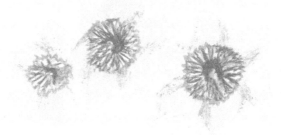

Some people like purple...
tingling with quiet energy.
Calm and peaceful and serene....

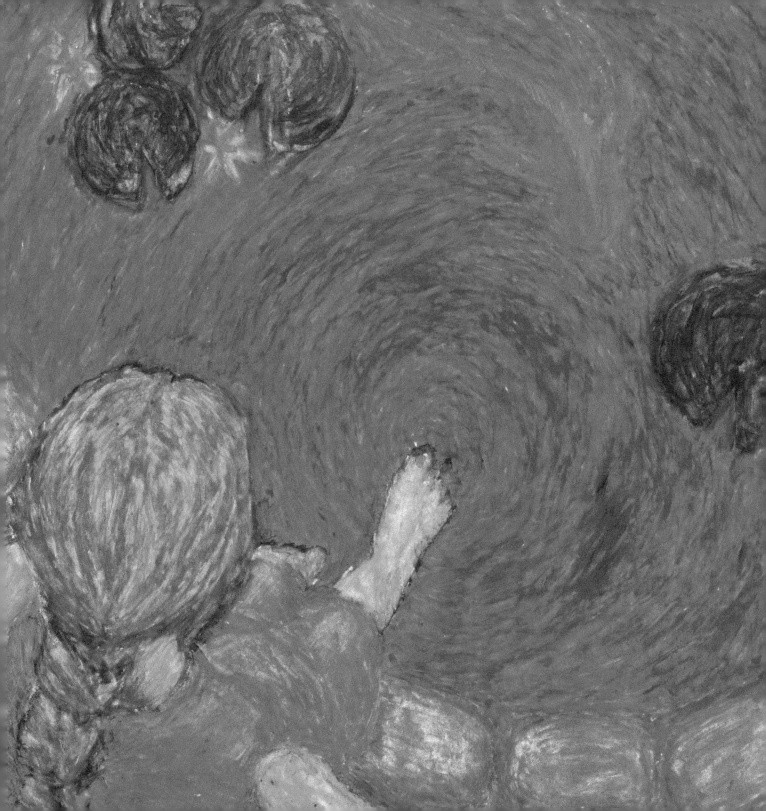

Some people love the turquoise ray...
that lovely color between green and blue,
in all its various shades.
Turquoise stones from the earth
and the color of the sea on a quiet day.

Maybe on some days you are
a glowing yellow person...

and the next day tranquil purple...

and then serene, life-filled green.

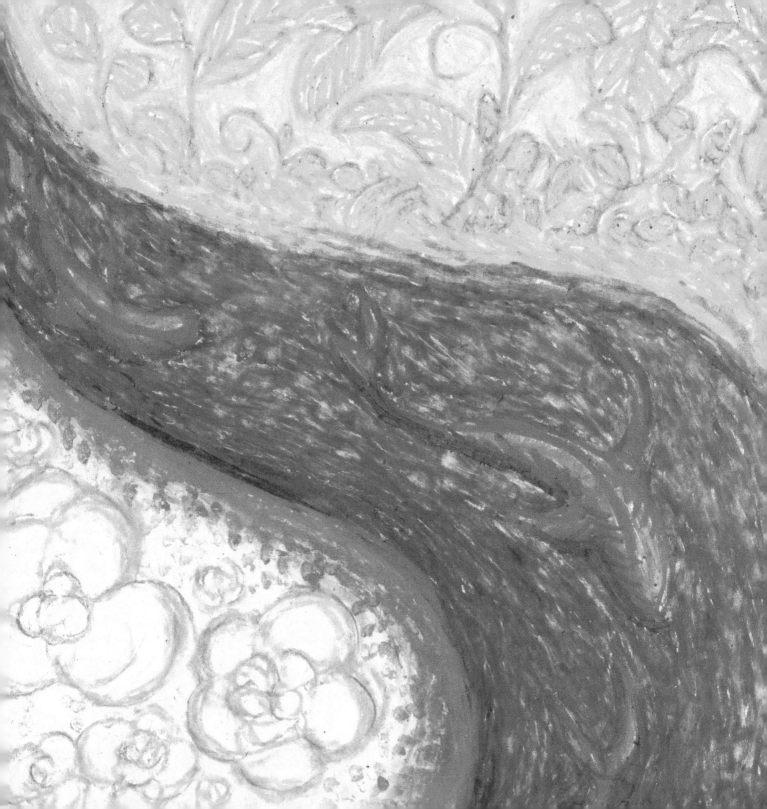

There are all kinds of us here
on our planet Earth—our lovely
blue-green planet, spinning in the sky.
It takes all kinds of us to make
the many combinations of light.

Birds singing...
sun setting over the mountains...
moon rising...
stars dancing.

I am glad there are so many different kinds of us and that we make so many beautiful pictures together, aren't you?

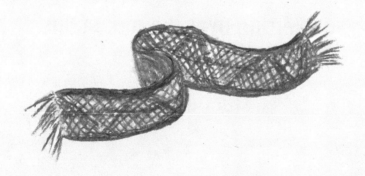

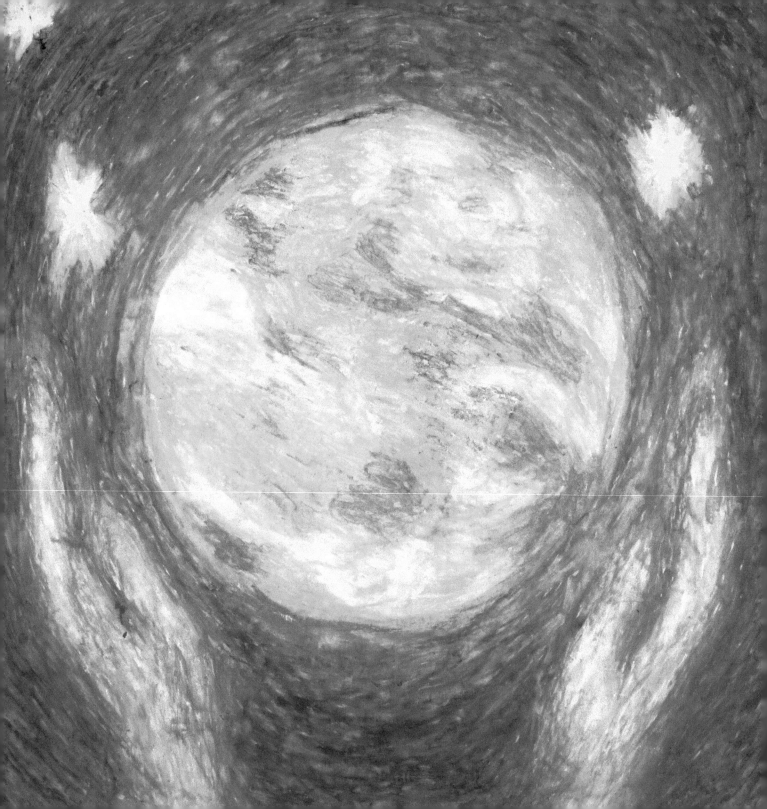

It's a beautiful, magical place,
this planet Earth...our home.

Margot Vance-Borland, MS, LPC, has been an energy worker, Reiki teacher and practitioner, and Hakomi Mind Body Therapist for over 33 years. She encourages her students and clients to go within themselves, and in some cases to find the images and colors that deeply resonate with them...for healing and spiritual alignment. Margot is thrilled to have worked on this book with her daughter Ari.

For more information, you can contact her at reikiwomyn@gmail.com or visit her website at www.seichimcenter.com.

Ari Vance-Borland is an artist and graphic designer living in Portland, Oregon. She likes playing with color and typography, picking blackberries, and snuggling her small children. Her favorite colors are blue and gray.

For more information, visit her website at arivanceborland.com, or find her @ari.vb.pdx.